A NOTE TO PARENTS

Nature offers ideal opportunities to share God with children, and this book can be a good starting point. After reading it, you might sit under the stars and talk about how God created the stars and the moon. Listen to bird calls and begin to recognize each one. Give thanks that God made the world in colors, not black and white.

Since young children think concretely, they often ask us why they can't see God. You might ask a child how we know when the wind blows. We don't see the wind, but we hear it, feel its coolness, and see what it does. In the same way, we don't see God, but we feel God is near us and hear and see what God has made.

— *Delia Halverson*

Delia Halverson is the consultant for *Family Time Bible Stories*. An interdenominational lecturer on religious education, she has written seven books, including *How Do Our Children Grow?*

Scripture sources: **Genesis 1:1-27**

FAMILY TIME
BIBLE
STORIES

IN THE BEGINNING

Retold by Mary Quattlebaum

Illustrated by Bryn Barnard

TIME
LIFE Kids™

ALEXANDRIA, VIRGINIA

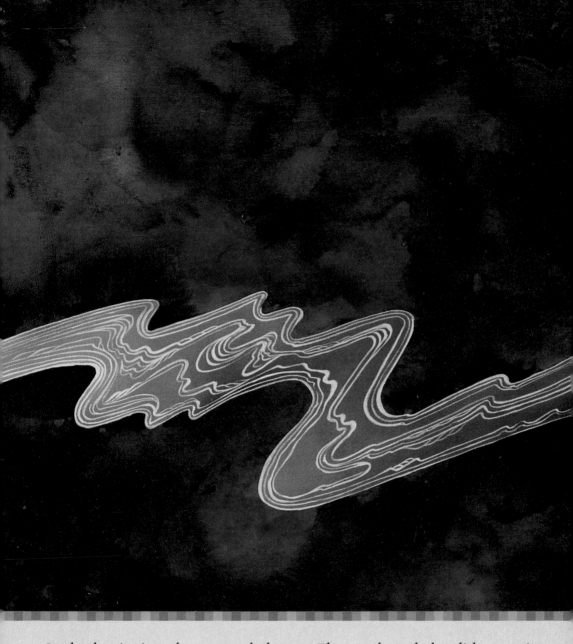

In the beginning, there was darkness. The earth and sky did not exist.

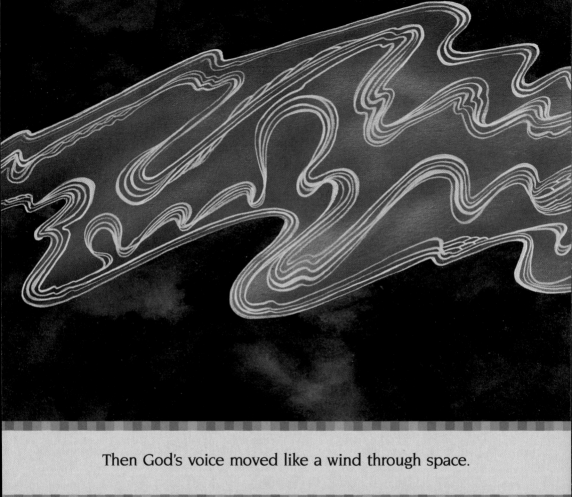

Then God's voice moved like a wind through space.

God said, "Let there be light," and the first light shone.

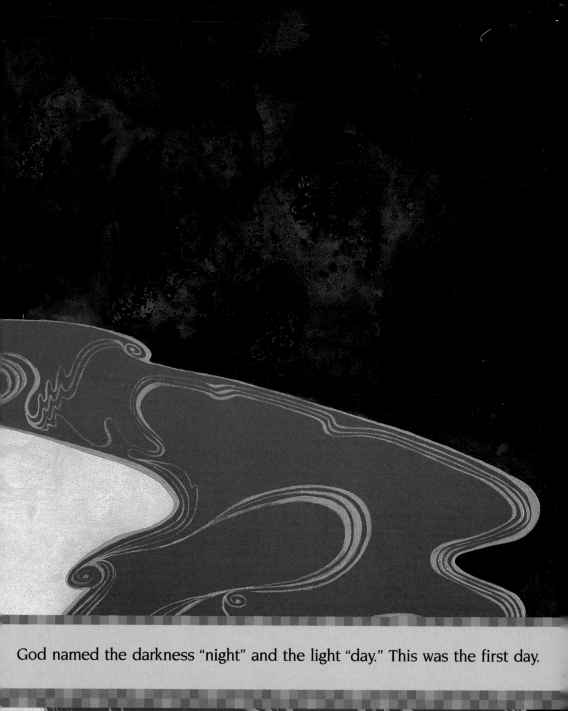

God named the darkness "night" and the light "day." This was the first day.

Then God created the sky.

The blue sky glowed above the dark waters. This was the second day.

From the waters, God created dry land.

God called the land "earth" and the water "seas."

"Let there be plants and trees," God said next.
Grass and flowering trees sprang into being.

Seeds sent out roots and grew. The earth filled with new green leaves and the sea with waving weeds. This was the third day.

God created the sun for day and the moon for night

and set each star in the sky.

"These great lights will mark the seasons," God said.

This was the fourth day.

Next God created big fish and small fish and every kind of bird. The seas

...lled with silvery life and the sky with singing birds. This was the fifth day.

"Let there be living creatures on the earth," God called. And animals raced through the grass and climbed the new trees.

Gazelles sprang into the air. Lizards napped on sun-warmed stones. Frogs hopped in moonlit mud.

Then God created one man and one woman.

Sitting up, they smiled at the busy world.

"Watch over the fish and birds," God told them.

"Take care of the sun and moon, the land and sea and sky. You may use these things, but you must also protect them." God blessed the man and woman. This was the sixth day.

On the seventh day, God rested. God looked at the man and woman, the bears and butterflies, the minnows, the whales, the plants.

One by one, God counted the stars.

The world stretched out, a beautiful place.

And God saw that it was good.

TIME-LIFE KIDS®

Staff for FAMILY TIME BIBLE STORIES

Managing Editor:	Patricia Daniels
Art Director:	Susan K. White
Publishing Associate:	Marike van der Veen
Editorial Assistant:	Mary M. Saxton
Senior Copyeditor:	Colette Stockum
Production Manager:	Marlene Zack
Quality Assurance Manager:	Miriam Newton

First printing. Printed in U.S.A.   Published simultaneously in Canada.

Time Life Inc. is a wholly owned subsidiary of THE TIME INC. BOOK COMPANY.

TIME-LIFE is a trademark of Time Warner Inc. U.S.A.
School and library distribution by Time-Life Education,
P.O. Box 85026, Richmond, VA 23285-5026.
For subscription information, call 1-800-621-7026.

Library of Congress Cataloging-in-Publication Data

Quattlebaum, Mary.
In the beginning / retold by Mary Quattlebaum. p. cm.—(Family time bible stories)
Summary: Retells the classic Bible story of the creation from the book of Genesis.
ISBN 0-7835-4627-0
1. Bible stories, English—O.T. Genesis. 2. Creation—Biblical teaching—Juvenile literature. [1. Bible stories.—O.T. 2. Creation.] I. Title. II. Series.
BS651.Q84 1995   95-25283
222'.1109505— dc20   CIP
                                                AC